WOYOKA

by Mel Boring

DILLON PRESS, INC.
MINNEAPOLIS, MINNESOTA

Dillon Press, Inc., 500 South Third Street
Minneapolis, Minnesota 55415

Printed in the United States of America

Library of Congress Cataloging in Publication Data

Boring, Mel, 1939–
  Wovoka.

  (The Story of an American Indian; 32)
  SUMMARY: A biography of the Paiute messiah whose vision of a
land free from white domination led to the Ghost Dance religion and
was ultimately shattered by the Wounded Knee Massacre.
    1. Wovoka, 1856 (ca.)–1932—Juvenile literature. 2. Indians of
North America—Religion and mythology—Juvenile literature.
3. Wounded Knee Creek, Battle, of, 1890—Juvenile literature.
4. Paiute Indians—Biography—Juvenile literature. [1. Wovoka, 1856
(ca.)–1932. 2. Paiute Indians—Biography. 3. Indians of North
America—Biography] I. Title.
E99.P2W614   970.004'97 [B] [92]   80-24003
ISBN 0-87518-179-1

WOVOKA

As a boy in Nevada's Mason Valley, Wovoka grew up at
a time when white settlers were taking over the
homeland of his people, the Paiute Indians. Like many
Paiutes, Wovoka went to work for the whites as a ranch
hand, but he did not lose touch with his Paiute heritage.
In 1887 and again in 1889, he had trance visions which
he revealed to his people. Wovoka said that he had been
to the land of the dead and had returned with a message
from the Great Spirit. All Indians must dance, he said,
and soon the white people would be swept away by a
great flood. Dead Indians would be made alive again,
and the Indian people would inherit the new earth, free
from white domination.

Before long 60,000 Indians from more than 30 tribes
joined in Wovoka's dance, including the Sioux, who
called it the Spirit Dance. Frightened white officials
called it the Ghost Dance and called for soldiers to stop
it before an Indian uprising began. In 1890 the Indians'
faith in Wovoka's teachings was shattered when the U.S.
Army captured a group of Sioux Ghost Dancers. In
what became known as the Wounded Knee Massacre,
300 Sioux men, women, and children were killed by
soldiers who were afraid of their captives and the Ghost
Dance. The Sioux nation, and, in a sense, the hopes and
dreams of all American Indians died at Wounded Knee.

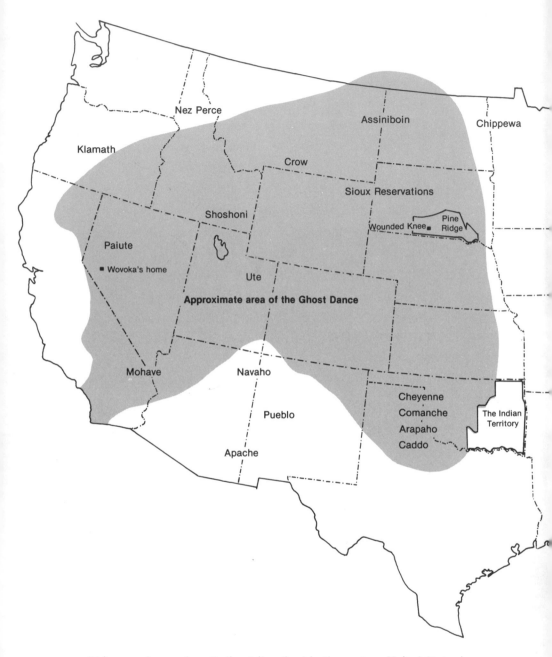

Klamath

Nez Perce

Assiniboin

Chippewa

Crow

Sioux Reservations

Shoshoni

Wounded Knee ■ Pine Ridge

Paiute

■ Wovoka's home

Ute

Approximate area of the Ghost Dance

Mohave

Navaho

Cheyenne

Comanche

Arapaho

Caddo

The Indian Territory

Pueblo

Apache

This map shows where Indian tribes lived in the western United States in 1890. The shaded area on the map shows how far Wovoka's dance spread from his home in Mason Valley.

Contents

Wovoka's Mason Valley homeland looked much like this Great Basin scene.

CHAPTER I

Journey To The Land
Of The Dead

In 1887 a horse-drawn wagon rolled slowly across the flat Nevada desert. Here and there, its wheels lumbered over clumps of sagebrush, jolting the wagon. Up on the seat, the driver barely felt the jolts. Wovoka was thinking about the great vision of peace he had received the day before. At the end of his ride, Paiute Indians from all over Mason Valley would be waiting to hear about his strange journey to the land of the dead.

Wovoka's home, Mason Valley, lay sixty miles south of Virginia City. Virginia City was a mining boom town that had sprung up when Wovoka was a boy. Before the white settlers had come, Mason Valley was a flat, narrow strip of sage prairie that seemed cut off from the rest of the world. To the east it was walled in by the Wassuk Mountains. To the west the lofty peaks of the Sierra Nevada towered over the dry lands below. To the south rose Mount Grant, the sacred mountain of the Paiutes. And above the valley was the bright blue, cloudless desert sky.

The white settlers of Mason Valley called Wovoka a dreamer. His own people, however, respected him for his strong awareness of the spirit world. As Wovoka's wagon jostled its way across the harsh desert land, his thoughts remained in the land of the unseen.

Wovoka pulled the wagon up at the edge of a clearing where Paiute ceremonies were held. A large circle had been cleared of sagebrush. Edging the circle were a few brush huts which had been built for the important guests. In one of the huts there would be private talks with the man whom the Paiutes looked to more and more as their leader. When evening came, they would sit at Wovoka's feet to hear about his vision.

A few days before, when Wovoka had fallen into a trance, he lay still on his bed as if he were dead. The people of his tiny village had tried to waken him. Burning sticks were pressed against his feet. Food was forced into his mouth by his wife, who feared he would starve. But none of their attempts had roused him from his deathlike sleep.

Then, just the day before, Wovoka had slowly awakened. His people were stunned. They thought he had died. Yet he had returned from death. Now, they believed, he would have an important message for them from the spirit world.

Every Paiute was eager to hear Wovoka's message. For twenty years white settlers had been moving into Mason Valley, taking the best land for farming and leaving the poorest for the Paiutes. The places where the Indian people had gathered desert plants and hunted animals had been taken away. The Paiutes were hungry for words of hope.

At last the time came for Wovoka to tell about his vision. Under the star-filled desert sky, he spoke to the

Paiutes in the clearing beside a blazing fire. In the trance, he told them, he had gone to the land of their ancestors, whom the Paiutes called the Grandfathers. It was a mysterious land of beauty and peace. There Indians of all tribes lived together along with the animals of the earth. In that faraway land there was no pain or disease. And there Indians were free from the power of white people.

Excitement grew among Wovoka's listeners. They longed to go where Wovoka had gone—to see what he had seen. His face glowed as he told them how he had wanted to stay in that land of peace. The Grandfathers, however, had told him to return to the living Paiutes. He was to tell them that the spirits of their ancestors were alive. They must not cry when loved ones died.

The Grandfathers had promised Wovoka that someday the living Paiutes would join them in that land of happiness. Jesus, said Wovoka, was coming to earth again. Only this time he was coming to the Indian people. While the people were waiting, they must not lie, steal, or quarrel. They must love one another and live in peace with the white people. To prepare for the coming of the new world, Wovoka gave the Paiutes a gift from the land of the Grandfathers. The gift was a dance.

Dancing the dance, said Wovoka, would bring the world of peace to earth. And it would make their waiting a time of joy. First, he taught the people a song to sing as they danced.

The whirlwind! The whirlwind!

The snowy earth comes gliding.

To the Paiutes the meaning of the song was clear. The earth would be swept away by a great storm. Then a new earth, clean as fresh-fallen snow, would appear. There all Indians would be free and happy and forever young.

Next, Wovoka taught them the dance. The Paiutes joined hands around the fading fire. Wovoka started the circle moving to the left in a simple, shuffling side step. The dancers barely lifted their feet and slid one step to the left. Then they drew their right feet up beside the left. Soon those outside the circle joined in until everyone was dancing.

The dance was as simple as the song they sang. But this was a special dance. Feelings were released that many Paiutes had long held inside—feelings of freedom.

Before Wovoka taught his people the new dance, dancing had been only a small part of Paiute life. For thousands of years, the people had little time for such activities. Food was scarce for the Paiutes and for the other Indians who lived in the Great Basin. Most of their time was spent searching for food in this harsh desert land.

For the Paiutes the Great Basin was a vast area which stretched from what are now the states of Wyoming and Idaho to Colorado and westward across Utah and Nevada. It was made of scattered ranges of mountains which rose from flat, desertlike valleys and plains. Dry winds blowing eastward from the Sierra Nevada took away what little moisture there was in the basin. Little grew there except sagebrush and cacti.

Some of the Paiutes lived on the shores of Pyramid and Walker lakes in what is now western Nevada. These people could catch fish and gather water plants to eat. Most, however, lived out in the barren desert. They were called "Diggers" by the white settlers because they used sticks to dig up plants for food. The whites looked upon the Diggers as not much better than animals.

Much of the Paiutes' food came from desert plants. From the tiny seeds to the dry roots, the desert people made use of all the parts of more than one hundred plants. Armed with digging sticks and clubs, they found enough food to survive in a land where most people would have starved.

In addition to the desert plants, the Paiutes hunted rabbits, gophers, birds, desert rats, mice, and lizards. A rare deer, antelope, or mountain sheep was a special treat. To trap rabbits the people used a hunting method called the drive. First long sagebrush fences were piled up to form a corral with a gate on one end. Women and children drove rabbits into the corral where they were clubbed by the men. At times the people hunted with bows and arrows. But the drive was their favorite hunting method.

Grasshoppers were also food for the Paiutes. These insects were driven with fire. Sagebrush was set afire in a large circle, driving the hoppers toward the center. There they were roasted and eaten.

Since the Paiutes did not have the means to store food, everything was eaten at once. When the food in one area was used up, they moved on. One family could use up all sources of food within several miles in a few weeks. In warmer seasons the people climbed to higher ground in search of food. When the weather turned colder, they moved to the low-lying regions. Each Paiute knew where and when to find the many kinds of foods in the dry lands of the Great Basin.

The people traveled in small groups of a few families.

Sometimes several small groups came together for a hunting drive or for spending the short, bitter winter in a sheltered spot. Then as many as fifteen families camped together. In the winter there was time for telling stories and dancing. Most of the time, however, the Paiutes were on the move, searching for food.

Paiute homes were called wickiups. These were small shelters which could be built or taken apart quickly. First a hole was scooped out of the ground to make a firm, level floor. A frame of sticks was set up to support the cone-shaped shelter. When the frame was covered with mats of sagebrush or rushes, it formed a house just large enough for one family. To complete the wickiup, a fire pit was dug in the floor, and a smokehole was cut in the roof. Food was cooked by boiling water with hot stones in watertight baskets.

Because there were long seasons of hot weather, the Paiutes needed few clothes. Sometimes the men wore breechclouts, while the women wore fringed aprons of milkweed fiber. During the cold winters the people wore leggings and sandals. Some wore rabbitskin robes and basket hats, too.

The small, wandering Paiute groups had no military or political leaders. At times they were led by the "talkers," the oldest and wisest men. Certain people also became shamans, or medicine men. Inspired by dreams, they cured sickness and performed ceremonies to aid in hunting drives.

When white settlers settled in the harsh Great Basin lands, most of the ten thousand Indians who lived there fled. They had neither the time nor the strength to fight.

A Paiute wickiup could be built or taken apart quickly.

At first there were not enough whites to do all the work on the ranches in places like Mason Valley. Some Paiutes, including Wovoka, went to work for the settlers to keep from starving to death. They took on white customs such as dress. Inside, however, they were angry at the white settlers for taking over their homeland.

The Paiutes were becoming servants for the white settlers. From every side they were being crowded out, and there was no place left for them to go. Theirs was the sad plight shared by American Indians all over the United States.

The dance Wovoka taught the Paiutes that night in 1887 gave them a feeling of hope. It promised that one day, their homeland would be theirs again. They would share it with all their Indian ancestors. There was great power in the dance brought to them from the land of the dead by the young Paiute leader.

CHAPTER II

The Uprooted Paiutes

The first white people in Paiute memory had appeared in the Great Basin while Wovoka's father, Tavibo, was growing up. They were trappers on their way to the far west where there were many beavers and other fur-bearing animals. During the 1820s and 1830s, more and more trappers made the journey west. The whites did not understand the way of life of the Paiutes. They looked upon them as "savages." Sometimes the trappers took potshots at the Diggers for sport.

After many years of unfair treatment, the Paiutes began to defend themselves. During the 1840s they fought back against some of the wagon trains which traveled through their lands. By the time Wovoka was born in 1856, gold had been discovered in California. The flow of white newcomers had turned into a stampede. Still, the whites were only passing through. No one wanted to settle on the barren lands of the lowly Paiutes.

Suddenly, in 1859, gold and silver strikes brought white fortune hunters rushing into Mason Valley. The whites ripped up the plants that the Paiutes depended upon for food. They killed the few deer, antelope, and other game which the Paiutes needed to survive. Soon starvation

Many white wagon trains traveled west through Paiute lands.

began to take its toll of Paiute people.

When the gold and silver ran out, most of the miners left the Great Basin. Some of them, however, stayed on to settle there. This first group of white settlers was joined by ranchers who came to Mason Valley because its flat sagebrush prairie was suited to grazing. The first ranchers came to the valley in 1863. Seven years later the valley was dotted with ranches. The ranchers took over Paiute water holes, claimed the lands that the Paiutes needed for food, and trampled on the sacred grounds of Paiute ancestors.

Wovoka's father was a respected leader among the Mason Valley Paiutes. He was a shaman who became known as a "talker." When the white settlers began to seize their lands, the people looked to Tavibo for leadership. He went up into the mountains to seek the guidance of the Grandfathers.

When Tavibo came down from the mountains, he told his people that he had had a vision. In the vision, he said, the white settlers had been destroyed. Mason Valley had been given back to the Paiutes. Then Tavibo taught his people a dance which was like the one Wovoka would teach them years later.

As the son of a shaman, Wovoka was expected to follow in his father's footsteps. Watching Tavibo in the family wickiup, young Wovoka learned the duties of a shaman. As he was growing up, Wovoka became a lot like his father. Both liked being alone, and both spent much time in deep thought.

Nothing is known about Wovoka's mother or the part she played in his life. According to the Paiute way, she would have helped give Wovoka his name, which means "the cutter." Most likely this name had something to do with food gathering.

While young Wovoka was learning the ways of his people, the Paiutes were being forced to follow a new way of life. They were no longer free to roam the land in search of food. Many hung around white settlements where they might be able to find something to eat. Some went to work for the settlers at low-paying jobs to earn money to feed their families. Within a few years the Paiute homeland became a white ranch land.

Even the peaceful Paiutes sometimes took action against unfair treatment by the whites. When drunken miners kidnapped two Paiute women, their husbands raised a party to rescue them. The rescue was carried out without a shot being fired. The Paiutes did not try to punish the guilty white miners. Afterward the whites called the Paiutes' action an "Indian outrage." They organized a large group of miners and marched toward Pyramid Lake to wipe out the Indian camp. The Paiutes, armed mostly with bows and arrows, surprised the whites in a narrow pass. Led by a tribal elder known as Chief Winnemucca, they soundly defeated the whites and chased them away.

Several battles were fought between the Paiutes and the whites. In 1862 Winnemucca's forces were defeated by a large U.S. Army expedition. Chief Winnemucca met with James Nye, governor of the newly formed Nevada Territory. In return for their stolen land, the Paiutes were promised food, money, and other goods. The promises, however, were never kept.

By the time Wovoka was thirteen, white settlers ruled Mason Valley. Wovoka was beginning to understand what was happening to his people. Some of the Paiutes were forced to move to reservations on Pyramid Lake and the Walker River. Wovoka's family and most of his people lived in camps which they were allowed to set up close, but not too close, to the white settlements. There they could stay as long as the whites wanted them—as prisoners in their own land.

The Paiutes worked for the white settlers in spring and summer, the busiest times on the ranches. Their days were

Chief Winnemucca, who wore a bone through his nose to
show his rank in the tribe.

filled with dull tasks like housecleaning and woodcutting. In the fall and winter, the Paiutes attempted to return to their old way of life. They gathered the plants of the desert and tried to forget that their homeland was no longer theirs.

Unlike other Indians who lived near the whites, the Paiutes did not take on the settlers' harmful habits. They did, however, do some of the harmless things. For example, they began to dress like the whites. The Paiutes stayed away from the alcohol that many of the whites drank. Perhaps staying in their homeland kept them from the despair which drove other Indians to drink the white people's whiskey.

In 1870, when Mason Valley was filled with white settlers, Tavibo died. At fourteen Wovoka was an orphan. A white family named the Wilsons took him into their house and adopted him. They gave him a new home and new name—Jack Wilson. The white settlers of the valley would always know him by this name.

David and Mary Wilson were the first white family to settle in Mason Valley. Looking for ranch land, the Wilsons had moved west from Missouri in 1863. They chose the Paiutes' valley because of its rich bottomlands. The Walker River provided a steady water supply, and plenty of timber grew in the nearby foothills. The mountains that ringed the valley offered protection from the harsh desert winds.

The Wilsons built their home on the Pine Grove hunting ground of the Paiute grandfathers. A few years later, David Wilson and his brothers returned to Missouri and drove their cattle out to Nevada. By then other settlers had moved to Mason Valley, and the Paiutes were becoming the settlers' servants.

With fourteen seasons of Paiute life behind him, Wovoka was thrown all at once into the life of a white family. He became a ranch hand for the Wilsons. The husky young Paiute was made to feel at home on the ranch and in the family. The Wilson's oldest son, Bill, was about Wovoka's age, and the two became close friends. Bill helped Wovoka to find his way in the strange new world of the whites.

The Wilsons dressed Wovoka in white ranch clothes and cut his hair short. They spoke to him in English, which he learned to speak quickly. Soon Wovoka was sitting on a chair instead of squatting on the ground. He plowed the land which had belonged to his people for thousands of years. He branded cattle which grazed on the plants that the Paiutes had once used for food. And he cut wood from the hunting ground of the Paiute grandfathers.

At first Wovoka just watched what was going on in the Wilsons' home. He listened to them talk and heard their Bible reading and prayers at night. The story in the Bible of how the world was made puzzled him. It was not at all like the one he had heard from Tavibo. For the most part, however, Wovoka was impressed by the Christian religion. He liked the gentle yet powerful Jesus and his teachings about the power of God's love. Little by little, Wovoka was included in the Wilsons' home life. The Paiute Wovoka was becoming Jack Wilson.

To the Wilsons Wovoka seemed to be a gentle young man who sometimes daydreamed. Often he looked as if he was off in a world of his own. Even though he lived in the white world now, he did not forget what Tavibo had taught him. Wovoka never lost touch with the world of the spirit.

Most white settlers thought that Indians were lazy. In Mason Valley, however, the ranchers admired Wovoka for his hard work. For years Wovoka appeared to be happy with his work and his life with the Wilsons. Living among the settlers of Mason Valley was making him into a white man.

To his own people he was still Wovoka, the son of the shaman and talker, Tavibo. The Paiutes hoped that one day Wovoka would set them free from their bondage to the whites. Their hope—and his own Paiute roots—kept him from straying completely into the white way of life.

Was he Wovoka or Jack Wilson? Perhaps he himself did not know then. But time would tell him. And time was moving swiftly by.

CHAPTER III

Birth Of
A Dream

When Wovoka was twenty, he left the Wilson ranch and moved back into a Paiute wickiup. Though he still worked at the ranch, he no longer lived the life of Jack Wilson. The Paiute people were happy to see Wovoka return to them. And they were pleased that the son of Tavibo chose to marry a Paiute woman.

For the next ten years Wovoka lived a quiet life with his Indian wife. We do not know her name. Three children were born to the Paiute couple, and all three died at birth. Later two healthy children were born to them. Little is known about his day-to-day life during those ten quiet years.

While Wovoka appeared to be a quiet man on the outside, much was going on inside him. Ever so slowly, he was moving deeper into the silent world of the spirit. To a shaman the spirit world was very real and powerful. Wovoka turned to that world to find help for his troubled people.

As a boy Wovoka had begun to learn the ways of a Paiute shaman from his father. Tavibo had taught him how to forecast a successful hunt. Wovoka had learned to heal the sick, predict the weather, and cast out evil spirits.

Secrets of magic used by Paiute shamans were also passed on from father to son. Tavibo showed Wovoka how to make things disappear.

During the ten quiet years of Wovoka's life, the seeds of Tavibo's teaching grew inside him. Paiute suffering would end, Tavibo had said. The whites would be destroyed. A new world was coming in which Indian ancestors would come to life. Like Tavibo, Wovoka was preparing to lead the Paiutes' struggle for freedom.

Many other American Indians had faced the same struggle as the Paiutes. And, like Wovoka, Indian leaders had turned to the spirit world for help.

Early in the 1800s, white settlers were taking over the land from the Ohio Valley to the Great Lakes. At that time Indians from many tribes looked to two Shawnee leaders to lead them against the whites. Tecumseh and his brother, known as the Prophet, urged all Indians to join together. They asked the people to give up the evil ways they had learned from the whites and go back to the old ways. Then, said the two Shawnees, Indians would have the strength to take back their lands.

The Prophet believed that he had been to the spirit world. There, he said, he had been given a message to bring back to his people. He would open a new door for them and teach them a better way of life. All Indians, said the Prophet, should live together in peace on the land given to them by the Great Spirit. But they should not live with whites because their strength lay in the peaceful union of their own people.

The Prophet spoke through Tecumseh. Tecumseh was a powerful speaker and a bold leader who was respected by

Like Wovoka, the Prophet gave a message of hope to American Indians.

both Indians and whites. He led a union of warriors from thirty-two tribes against the Americans in the War of 1812. Finally Tecumseh was killed in battle. The movement led by the two great Shawnees came to an end.

Thousands of Indian warriors from many tribes fought under Tecumseh's leadership.

Another Indian leader with spiritual power was Smoholla, a Sahaptin. He rose to power in the Colombia River Plateau, north of the Great Basin, at about the time Wovoka was born. Among his followers were the Yakima, Klickitat, and Nez Perce Indians. Smoholla urged them to look to their gods for help against the whites.

Smoholla's followers were called "Dreamers." They could put themselves in a dreamlike trance. Afterward, the dreamers told of visions they had seen in the trance. In the visions, they said, Indians were getting back their stolen lands. These visions were much like those of Wovoka.

The Dreamers believed they lived in two worlds. In the earthly world, Indians faced trouble from whites. But in the world of the trance, their spirits left their bodies and entered the invisible spirit world. By putting themselves into a trance, they could get help from the spirits of their ancestors.

Wovoka carried on the tradition of Tavibo, the Prophet and Tecumseh, and Smoholla. The power of the spirit world, the turning back to Indian ways, and the trance vision—all became part of Wovoka's message to the Paiutes. And to them he added the teachings of the gentle yet powerful Christ which he had learned from the Wilsons.

Unlike the prophets before him, Wovoka made the dance the most important part of his message. The Paiutes must dance, he said, to bring on the new world. Wovoka called upon his people to dance every six weeks for four nights at a time. On the fourth night they were to keep dancing all night long. Then, on the morning of the fifth day, they were to bathe in the river. In this way the evil would be washed from their bodies.

Wovoka made a promise to his people. If they danced the sacred dance, all that the white people had taken away would be given back to them. Starting on that night in 1887, the Paiutes danced. Wovoka's ten quiet years had come to an end.

CHAPTER IV

The Day
The Sun Died

Two years went by. Every six weeks, the Paiutes danced for four nights as Wovoka had taught them. On the morning of the fifth day, they bathed in the river.

Then one day, the sun died.

To the Paiutes the sun was a living, godlike being. When an eclipse darkened the sun on January 1, 1889, Wovoka's people were afraid. An evil monster was attacking the sun, they said. Unless it was stopped, the sky monster would eat up the sun. The world would be plunged into darkness forever.

Bit by bit, the sun disappeared. The sky monster was eating only a small slice at a time. At first the Paiutes stood in silent shock, angrily squinting at the sun. Soon the sky was as dark as the fading light of sunset.

Wovoka did not see the sky monster attack the sun. He lay helpless on the floor of his wickiup. For days he had suffered from scarlet fever, one of the white people's diseases. It had struck many Paiutes—some had died. Wovoka was weak from the fever. His throat was raw and sore, and his lips were dry and cracked.

When the fever had first struck him, Wovoka had tossed and turned on the dirt floor. Sweat drenched his

The Paiutes were frightened by the eclipse of the sun.

body. Now, however, he lay still. Nearby his wife watched him closely. She was frightened because others less sick than her husband had died.

Outside, it grew darker as the sun became smaller and smaller. A low moaning had started among the people. Before long their sad wailing filled the air. Some of them shouted, trying to scare the monster away. Others shot arrows and threw stones toward the sky.

At last near darkness covered Mason Valley. To the Paiutes it seemed as if the sky monster had eaten the sun. They fought against its dying, but all their noise and arrows and stones could not bring it back. The life-giving sun had slipped away.

Inside the wickiup, Wovoka's life seemed to slip away, too. He showed no sign of hearing the noise outside. Once in a while, he whispered a few words about the spirit world. His wife could not understand them. By the far-off way he spoke, she thought he was in another world. She did not know if he was in a trance or was suffering from the fever.

Outside the Paiutes were silent again. The people shivered in the chilly darkness and stared at the sky. It seemed as if years had passed since the sky monster had begun to attack the sun. As the white people measured time, however, it had been less than ten minutes.

Suddenly a small sliver of the sun brightened the sky. The sliver turned into a wedge, and then into a quarter and a half. The people shouted for joy. The sky monster had been scared away!

In a few minutes the sun cast its full light and warmth on Mason Valley again. Inside the wickiup, Wovoka came back to life, too. He trembled, and his eyes fluttered open. His wife rushed outside to tell the people that Wovoka would live.

Wovoka rose and staggered to the doorway. The Paiutes did not know what to think. What, they asked him, was the meaning of the sun mystery? Wovoka was too weak to answer. He needed rest and food. After that, he promised, he would explain everything that had happened during the day the sun died.

Today an eclipse of the sun is no mystery. But to the Paiutes in 1889, it meant that something very important was going to happen to them. The people were eager to find out what Wovoka had learned during his sun trance.

A few days later, Wovoka called the Paiutes to the same clearing where he had taught them the dance-in-a-circle. A fire crackled in the center of the clearing. News of Wovoka's sun trance had reached other Paiutes at Walker Lake and beyond. From miles around they came to hear about the meaning of the sun mystery.

When everyone had arrived, Wovoka stood before the fire. He was no longer weak. Tall and broad shouldered, he towered over the people at his feet. On the day the sun died, Wovoka said, he had fallen asleep in the daytime. Just as in his earlier trance, he was taken up to the land of the Grandfathers. And this time, he had seen the Great Spirit!

In the land of the dead, Wovoka explained, he had seen all the Paiutes who had died. He had walked with them, and talked to them. They were playing games, dancing, and singing.

The Paiutes were moved by Wovoka's words. They

Wovoka explained the meaning of the sun mystery to the Paiutes.

pictured loved ones who had died of scarlet fever—mothers, fathers, brothers, and sisters—who were now alive and well.

In the spirit world, said Wovoka, animals roamed among the people in great numbers. The people were free like the wind. When it was cold, they journeyed to the warm valleys of the south. There, bubbling springs healed every sickness. When it grew warm again, they moved back into the mountains of the north.

Listening to Wovoka, the Paiutes remembered their own days of freedom. Before the coming of the white settlers, the people had roamed wherever they pleased. They longed to return to those good times.

On the day the sun died, said Wovoka, the Great Spirit told him a big secret—the secret of how the Paiutes would regain their homeland. One day soon, the Indian people would be taken up high above the mountains. There would be thunder and lightning. Below them the earth would rumble, and an earthquake would break the land into pieces. Then a great flood would sweep across the land below. All the white people would be destroyed by the earthquake and flood, but the Indians would not be harmed. High above the earth, the Paiutes would dance and sing with joy.

Just as the sun had been destroyed and made new, explained Wovoka, so would the earth. That was the meaning of the sun mystery. The white earth monsters who had swallowed up the land would be driven away like the sky monster. And a new earth would come down to cover the old.

All Indians who had ever died would come back alive.

Everyone would be young again. There would be no sickness, no dying. The new world would be greener, and all the people would have enough food to eat.

White people would have no part of the new world, said Wovoka. The new land would belong only to the Indians. He warned them not to tell the white settlers what was going to happen.

Wovoka said nothing about when the new world was going to come. By the way he spoke, however, the Paiutes were sure that it would not be long. Meanwhile, he told them, they were to go on working for the white settlers and not make trouble. They were to love one another and do what was right.

Wovoka warned his people that the new world would never come unless they danced. Only those who danced, he said, would be allowed to live there. Those who didn't dance would be burned up like firewood.

Finally, Wovoka gave the Paiutes two gifts—red paint and magpie feathers—which they were to wear during the dance. The sacred paint would keep away sickness until the new world came. When the earthquake shook the land, the magpie feathers would become wings to carry the people to safety high above.

After his sun trance, Wovoka had greater power over his people than ever. The sun trance had set him apart from the other Paiutes. From that day on, he was more than just a man to them. He was a prophet sent by the Great Spirit to rescue the Indian people from slavery to the whites in their own land.

CHAPTER V

The Dance Circle Grows

Inspired by Wovoka's vision of the new world, more and more Paiutes joined in the dance. The circle of dancers grew so large that the clearing had to be made bigger. Every six weeks, Paiutes streamed into Mason Valley from miles around. They danced with a fury in the hope that the new world would appear.

Wovoka gave the people a new song to sing with the dance.

> There is dust from the whirlwind,
> The whirlwind on the mountains.
> The rocks are ringing,
> They are ringing on the mountains.
> The whirlwind! The whirlwind!
> The snowy earth comes gliding.

Starting from Mason Valley, the dance spread like wildfire. Thirty miles east on the Walker Lake Reservation, Paiutes were dancing. Seventy miles north on the Pyramid Lake Reservation, the people were dancing. By the end of 1889, almost every Paiute was dancing. Soon, Indian leaders from many tribes heard about the coming of the new world. They made their way swiftly to the Paiute prophet and took the dance back to their people.

Wovoka's dance-in-a-circle spread north, east, south, and west all at once. The Shoshonis carried the dance west to the Washo and Pit River Indians of Nevada and California. Other Indians took the dance south to the Walapais, Mohaves, and Chemehuevis in the Arizona Territory. Even the timid "Mission" Indians of southern California joined in the dance.

North of Mason Valley, in Nevada and Idaho, other groups of Shosonis learned the dance. To the northeast, the dance spread among the Bannocks and Assiniboins. To the east the Utes began to dance in Utah and Colorado. The Arapahos and Cheyennes took the dance to the tribes of Wyoming and Montana. By early in 1890, Wovoka's message had set Indians dancing all over the West.

In that year the dance movement crossed the Rocky Mountains and spread south to the Indians in Kansas and Oklahoma. At that time part of Oklahoma was called Indian Territory. Thousands of Indians had been forced to move there from their homelands in other parts of the United States. Many were suffering in the dry, crowded lands of Indian Territory.

When these Indians heard Wovoka's message from their northern relatives, they began to dance. The Pawnees, Apaches, Kiowas, Wichitas, Caddos, and some Comanches joined in the dance. Like so many other American Indians, these once proud and free tribes were eager to see the coming of the new world.

By the fall of 1890, sixty thousand Indians from more than thirty tribes were dancing. From Kansas to California, and from the Dakotas to Oklahoma, the people followed Wovoka's teachings. Some Indians

Wovoka's dance as it was practiced by the Arapahos.

danced with such excitement that they fell into the dance circle unconscious. When they woke up, they told about visions of the new world much like Wovoka's. In other tribes only a few Indians joined in the dance. Some tribes, like the Navajos, did not dance at all.

Wovoka's dance gave hope to American Indians who had lost their lands, their homes, and in many cases, their families. Since the first white settlers arrived in the early 1600s, hunger, disease, and war had killed three-fourths of the Indians in the United States. By 1890 only about two hundred fifty thousand Indians were left. Most of these people lived on reservations in barren places far from their homelands. And there were more than one hundred whites for every one Indian.

Many of the remaining Indians were hungry or starving. The buffalo and wild horses were gone, the trees had been cut down, and streams were dry. Smallpox, scarlet fever, and other diseases brought by the whites had wiped out entire Indian towns. Some tribes had tried to fight against the whites, but all had lost. Now Indians who had lost hope found it once more in the dance that promised to bring a new world free of white people.

Wherever Indians learned the dance, they learned about Wovoka, too. By the end of 1890, his name was known by most Indians and many whites. Some of his followers called him the Indian Messiah, the son of God. Back in Mason Valley, however, Wovoka did not know how fast and how far the dance was spreading. He would have been surprised to know that two of the white people's inventions were helping to spread it.

One of these inventions was the school. The U.S. government had started schools to teach Indians to "walk the white man's road." In these schools young Indians learned to read and write English. When they finished, many could write letters to send to other Indians far away. These letters helped carry the message of Wovoka's dance from one tribe to another.

White-owned railroads also helped to spread the dance over long distances. Because railroads were built on Indian lands, railroad owners gave Indians free rides on most trains. To learn more about the dance, some Indians

These workers built a railroad through Plains Indian lands in 1877.

traveled hundreds of miles to Mason Valley on trains. There they heard Wovoka's message and saw his dance firsthand. Then they returned to their people to teach them the dance.

Each time the dance passed from tribe to tribe, it changed a little. The Indians who taught the dance to their people did not mean to change it. But the way of life of each tribe was not exactly the same. When one tribe learned the dance, the people made it fit their own ways. The Bannock dance was a bit different from the Paiute dance. And the Arapaho dance was not the same as the Bannocks'.

One change in the dance was made by the tribes of the Great Plains. The buffalo was very important to the way of life of the Plains Indians. Like the Paiutes, they believed that dancing would bring back their Indian ancestors. But they also believed that the dance would bring back all the buffalo that the white hunters had killed.

As it was passed from tribe to tribe, the name of the dance changed, too. Among many Shoshonis, the dance was called Everybody Dragging because of its shuffling steps. The Kiowas called it the Dance with Clasped Hands. In the Great Plains it was called the Spirit Dance since the people believed it had come from the Great Spirit.

Frightened white settlers called it the "Ghost Dance." It was not a dance of ghosts, but one of living people. Few settlers, however, had ever seen the dance. They were afraid the Indians were planning an armed uprising. In their fear they watched the Indians closely for any sign of trouble. White soldiers were sent out to be ready to put down a revolt by the Ghost Dancers.

The most important change in the dance was made among some Plains Indian tribes. War had always played a big part in their way of life. The Plains Indian dancers came to believe that a warlike struggle would be part of the coming of the new world. They danced to hasten the coming of the Indian Messiah. Soon, they believed, the Messiah would wipe the whites from the face of the earth. He had returned to earth to punish the whites for their wickedness to American Indians.

The Sioux Indians were the largest and most powerful group of Plains Indians. As in other Plains tribes, the dance appeared warlike among the Sioux. Some of the people even began to carry guns during the dance. Wovoka had not allowed the Paiutes to carry any weapons while they were dancing. For him the dance-in-a-circle was a dance of peace, not war. He said nothing about war to the Sioux and other Indians who came to him to learn about the dance. To his followers Wovoka gave this advice: "You must not fight. Do no harm to anyone. Do right always."

CHAPTER VI

Visitors From Across
The Rockies

Early in 1890, a special group of Indian visitors arrived in Mason Valley. They had traveled a thousand miles on foot and horseback and by train. Eleven of the thirty-four visitors had been sent by the Sioux. Their party was led by Short Bull and Kicking Bear. In Mason Valley the Sioux met hundreds of other Indians who had come from far and near to see the prophet Wovoka.

The visitors from across the Rockies had been in Mason Valley three days before they saw the person they called the Messiah. First they learned the sacred dance by dancing from sundown until late at night. Then Wovoka appeared to speak to them.

In the beginning, said the Paiute prophet, God made the earth. Later he sent Christ to earth to teach the people about God's love for them. The white people had treated him so badly, however, that he had gone back to heaven. Soon, said Wovoka, Jesus would return to earth as an Indian. He would make all things as they were before the coming of the white people.

Wovoka told his listeners that the new world would come during the next spring when the grass was knee-high. All white people would be drowned. While the waves of

Short Bull, a leader of the Sioux who came to Mason Valley to learn the dance.

new earth covered the old, Indians who danced would be taken up safely into the air. Then they would be set down in the new world where only Indians would live. Sweet grass, running water, and trees would blanket the new land.

Wovoka's prediction about the coming of the new world excited the Sioux most. They had been troubled by white settlers for more than forty years. Once they had roamed freely all over the northern Great Plains. But in 1851, when the whites wanted to open a road to the west,

Kicking Bear was eager to hear Wovoka's message of hope.

the Sioux were forced to give up part of their lands. At that time the tribe was promised that the northern plains would be theirs "for all time." Like most white promises to the Indians, this one was not kept for long.

In 1865 white settlers wanted a shorter road to Montana Territory. It was planned to run along the Powder River, right through the best Sioux hunting grounds. The Sioux would have to give up land they had been promised "for all time." Unlike the Paiutes, however, the Sioux did not try to move out of the white people's way. The fight for Sioux land was on!

The U.S. Army made the first move by building forts along the planned route of the Powder River road. Building the forts, the army thought, would protect the road builders. The Sioux fought back against the white invaders. By 1867 the fighting had come to a standstill. Sioux warriors had trapped the soldiers inside their forts. The U.S. government decided that the best way to get the Sioux to leave their land was a treaty.

By the terms of the treaty, the Sioux were crowded into a reservation in what is now the western part of South Dakota. This reservation was less than one-fifth the size of the former Sioux homeland. In return, the whites promised to give up the building of the the Powder River road. That land would be reserved as a Sioux hunting ground. Also, the whites promised to supply beef, flour, and blankets to the reservation.

Many Sioux leaders refused to sign the treaty. These "non-treaty" Indians went on living outside the reservation. Still, there was no fighting until the whites who supplied food to the Sioux began cheating them. The Indians were receiving much less than they had been promised in the treaty. The beef was spoiled, the flour moldy, and the blankets moth-eaten. And worse yet, the Northern Pacific Railroad was about to cut right through Sioux territory!

To add to all these problems, white prospectors discovered gold on the Sioux reservation. In 1875 thousands of gold seekers rushed to the Black Hills. White officials tried to buy more land from the Sioux, but they refused to give it up. Fighting broke out once more.

The U.S. government ordered all Sioux to move to the

To the Sioux the Black Hills were sacred lands.

reservation. Thousands of Indians refused to leave their hunting grounds. The army sent a force of soldiers to trap these non-treaty Indians and force them onto the reservation.

In June 1876, Colonel George Custer led 265 U.S. soldiers into a fight with 2500 Sioux warriors. The foolhardy Colonel Custer and his men were killed. This battle, known as Custer's Last Stand, was a great victory for the Sioux. Before long, however, thousands more U.S. troops moved in to fight the Sioux warriors. By October the Indians were trapped and were forced to surrender. Three thousand Sioux managed to flee to Canada. The rest moved onto the reservation.

When the fighting ended, white settlers moved in to seize more Sioux land. In 1877 the Black Hills were lost to gold miners. Railroads crossing the Sioux reservation took away still more land. And part of the reservation was taken by North and South Dakota when the two states were formed in 1889.

During the 1880s the remaining buffalo were killed by white hunters. In 1889 lack of rain wiped out the Sioux food crops. That winter a measles plague killed hundreds of Sioux children. Food supplies from the U.S. government were cut in half. When Wovoka spoke to the visitors from across the Rockies, the Sioux were angry and restless. They listened eagerly to Wovoka's message of hope, and they believed that what he said was true. They could hardly wait for the coming of the new world to set them free.

Short Bull, Kicking Bear, and the other Sioux left Mason Valley in the spring of 1890. Wovoka gave them

The Pine Ridge agency in 1891.

red dance paint and magpie feathers to take back across the mountains. The Sioux traveled swiftly back to their people so that they could report Wovoka's message and teach them the dance.

Most of the Sioux lived near the six reservation agencies where supplies were handed out. The first Sioux to begin dancing were at the westernmost agency, Pine Ridge. Red Cloud, the great Sioux warrior, was the leader there. Next Short Bull started the dance at the Rosebud agency, where the people were led by Spotted Tail. Kicking Bear taught

Red Cloud led the Sioux at the Pine Ridge agency.

the dance to the Sioux at the Cheyenne River agency. The
Sioux at the Standing Rock agency were the last to learn
the dance. At first their leader, the famous Sitting Bull,
did not dance. But he invited Kicking Bear to teach his
people. All over Sioux country, the people danced for the
return of their land and their way of life.

Twenty thousand Sioux were dancing, singing, and
praying. Some fell into a trance and told of talking to the
dead. For many Sioux the dance turned into a bitter
protest against the whites' destruction of Indian life. What

Wovoka had started as a dance of happiness became a dance of anger. The Sioux looked to the next spring for revenge against the whites.

White settlers became fearful because they did not understand the dance. At the Pine Ridge agency, soldiers were sent out to stop the dancing. The Pine Ridge Sioux raised their guns. If necessary, they would defend the dance with their lives. The soldiers withdrew, and the tensions mounted.

When the Sioux at Standing Rock began to dance, Sitting Bull warned Kicking Bear that the whites might try to stop it. The Sioux leader wanted to protect his people. Kicking Bear replied that no harm would come to them if they wore sacred dance shirts.

The Sioux at Pine Ridge were the first to wear the dance shirts. The men wore shirts made of flour sacks or buckskin, and the women wore dresses made of the same material. Each male dancer painted a different sign on his shirt: the sun, the moon, the morning star, or the buffalo, eagle, or turtle. The dancers believed that the shirts would protect them from all harm.

Some of Wovoka's Paiutes had worn such shirts, but he did not approve. The Paiutes, said Wovoka, did not need the shirts. They were not to show anger. All they needed to do was dance and sing. The Great Spirit would do the rest. The Sioux, however, were far away, and Wovoka could not tell them that the shirts were not truly a part of the dance.

By the fall of 1890, so many Sioux were dancing that other activities stopped. Indian schools had no students. Trading stores were empty. No work was being done on

A Ghost Dance shirt worn by a Plains Indian.

the Sioux farms. The U.S. government agent at Pine Ridge asked for help from Washington, D.C. "Indians are dancing in the snow and are wild and crazy," he wrote. "We need protection, and we need it now."

Most whites believed that the dance was stirring up Indian anger. They wanted to stop it before it grew into an uprising. They failed to understand that the Sioux were angry long before they learned about the dance. Stolen lands, broken treaties, and spoiled food had made the

Three thousand Sioux fled to the Badlands to dance in freedom.

Sioux angry. The dance was merely a way to express that anger.

That fall the U.S. government issued an order: stop the Ghost Dance! Kicking Bear was arrested for teaching Sitting Bull's people to dance. Porcupine, a Cheyenne leader, was also taken into custody for teaching the dance among the Sioux. The more the whites tried to stop the dancing, the harder the Sioux danced. The people came to believe that the dance shirts they wore were bulletproof. They did not worry about the white soldiers that were marching toward the Sioux reservation.

Some Sioux leaders took their people away from the agencies to dance in freedom. Short Bull led three thousand Sioux into the area known as the Badlands north of Pine Ridge. Big Foot led six hundred of his people out to Deep Creek, away from the Cheyenne River. In spite of the wintry weather, the Sioux put on their dance shirts and danced until late at night. Contrary to what the white people believed, the Indians were neither wild nor crazy. They simply believed in a dream. And that dream was all they had left.

By November tensions between the Sioux and the whites had nearly reached the breaking point. Three thousand U.S. Army troops took command of all the Sioux agencies. There they began to arrest the people on the list of Sioux "troublemakers" made up by the Indian agents.

In Mason Valley Wovoka's people danced peacefully. The Paiutes did not wear dance shirts or carry guns. There were no soldiers closing in on them. Their dance seemed as different from the Sioux dance as peace is from war.

And the spring of 1891 was only a few months away.

CHAPTER VII

Last Stop At
Wounded Knee

When the U.S. Army took over the Sioux agencies, most of the dancing stopped. White leaders decided that it was a good time to arrest the "troublemakers." Sitting Bull was first on their list. He had allowed his people to dance, and he had even begun dancing himself. It made no difference to the whites that Sitting Bull had stopped dancing when the order had been given to stop. Some white officials at the Sioux agencies were out for revenge against him.

Their chance came when many of Sitting Bull's people refused to stop dancing. Major James McLaughlin, the Indian agent at Standing Rock, ordered Sitting Bull arrested. He planned to use the Indian police force at the agency instead of white soldiers. That way, he hoped, there would be no trouble.

The arrest was carried out on the cold, wintry morning of December 15. Before daybreak, the Indian police officer Bull Head arrived at Sitting Bull's home along with forty-three of his men. They rushed in, woke Sitting Bull, and told him he was under arrest. The Sioux leader did not resist. While he was getting dressed, his horse was being saddled by one of the policemen.

Sitting Bull, the great Sioux leader.

As the police led their prisoner out of the cabin, they were met by more than one hundred fifty angry Sioux who blocked their way. One of them, Catch the Bear, told the police they would never make it out of the camp alive. Bull Head spoke quietly to Sitting Bull, who was holding back now. Sitting Bull refused to move.

Suddenly one of the police, Red Tomahawk, shoved Sitting Bull from behind. Catch the Bear pulled a rifle from beneath his blanket and shot Bull Head in the side. As the police chief fell, he fired back, hitting Sitting Bull. In the next instant Red Tomahawk shot Sitting Bull in the head and killed him. A wild fight broke out between the Sioux and the police. Only the arrival of the U.S. cavalry saved the police from being killed by the furious Sioux.

When the calvary joined the battle, Sitting Bull's people were outnumbered and outgunned. Some of them fled to the Cheyenne River agency south of Standing Rock. There they would be protected by Hump and Big Foot, the leaders of the Cheyenne River Sioux.

With Sitting Bull dead, the whites thought Hump was the most troublesome Sioux leader. He was next in line to be arrested in the drive to stamp out the Ghost Dance. Rather than fight, however, Hump surrendered with his people at Fort Bennett, south of the Cheyenne River. Some of Sitting Bull's people surrendered with him. But others slipped away to join Big Foot.

Big Foot danced along with his Sioux followers. He believed strongly in Wovoka's promised new world. When Big Foot heard about the death of Sitting Bull, he led his people to the Pine Ridge agency. There he hoped to ask protection of Red Cloud and find shelter from the deepening fury of the Dakota winter.

U.S. Army troops chased the Sioux heading toward Pine Ridge. In the bitter cold, Big Foot caught pneumonia and had to be carried in a wagon. The cavalry caught up with the Sioux at Porcupine Creek, about thirty miles from Pine Ridge. Major Samuel Whitside ordered the prisoners taken to a cavalry camp at Wounded Knee Creek, just north of the agency.

Big Foot was moved to an army ambulance to make his trip more comfortable. His 350 Sioux followers were herded along like cattle. The soldiers planned to take their guns away at the Wounded Knee camp. Then the Sioux would be forced to march to the military prison at Omaha. Nearly 500 soldiers took charge of the 120 Sioux warriors and 230 women and children.

The captives arrived at Wounded Knee in the bone-chilling cold of dusk on December 28. Army leaders decided to wait until the next morning to disarm the Sioux warriors. During the night the troops surrounded the captives. Four large Hotchkiss guns were set up on a rise, overlooking the Sioux tipis. The guns could pour out fifty explosive shells per minute, and each of the shells could carry for two miles. The army was taking no chances with the Ghost Dancers.

For both the Sioux and the soldiers, it was a long, cold night. To celebrate the capture of Big Foot, the soldiers broke open a keg of whiskey. The Sioux shivered and waited to see what would happen next. They still believed that the whites would be destroyed when spring came. At this moment, however, they were afraid of what the soldiers might do with them.

The U.S. Army camp at Wounded Knee in 1891.

At eight o'clock the next morning, a bugle blast roused
the Sioux from an uneasy sleep. The Sioux men were
called forward and ordered to give up their guns. A few
came forward, but not enough to satisfy the army leaders.
They ordered the soldiers to ransack the Sioux tipis to
search for more guns. When no more arms were found,
the captives were ordered to remove their blankets for a
person-to-person search.

Yellow Bird told the other Sioux not to take off their blankets. Bullets would not hurt them, he said. The Sioux medicine man shuffled back and forth, dancing the forbidden Ghost Dance. From the edge of the camp, the Sioux women and children watched their husbands and fathers helplessly. Dozens of weary soldiers watched uneasily from a short distance away.

One by one, the soldiers stripped the Indians of their blankets. When they disrobed Black Coyote, they found him clutching a new rifle. It had cost him dearly, and he didn't want to give it up. The angry soldiers grabbed for the gun. Black Coyote raised it over his head out of reach. Furious, the soldiers pulled his arms down. When they did, the gun went off.

The shot was answered instantly by a blast of gunfire from the soldiers all around the camp. A split second later—in spite of their dance shirts—half of the Sioux warriors lay dead or wounded on the cold ground. Big Foot, who was lying sick in his bed, was one of the first to be killed.

Hand-to-hand fighting broke out between the soldiers and the Sioux warriors who were left. Then the huge Hotchkiss guns poured out a firestorm of exploding shells from the hilltop, killing both the Sioux and the soldiers nearby. Violent anger seized the gunners. Out of control, they senselessly killed men, women, and children.

Some of the Sioux scrambled up a dry creekbed to the west of the camp. Mothers grabbed their small children and ran for their lives. Long after it was clear that the Sioux were beaten, soldiers on horseback chased and gunned down the fleeing Indians. Sioux mothers were

Many Sioux died at Wounded Knee.

slaughtered as they tried to cover their children with their own bodies. Afterwards, the bodies of the massacred Indians were found scattered along the frozen ground for two miles.

Finally, the shooting ended. More than one-half of the Sioux were killed in the fighting. Many others were wounded so badly that they died soon afterward in the cold. Of the 350 Sioux, about 300 died in the Wounded

Knee massacre, and most of the 50 survivors were badly wounded. Only 25 whites were killed—most of them by their comrades' own bullets!

At dusk the soldiers returned with their wounded to the Pine Ridge agency. There they were treated at once by army doctors. The wounded Sioux were left outside in an open wagon until a place could be found for them. At last they were bedded down in the hay in the church chapel, where the Christmas tree still stood. Their torn and bleeding bodies shivered in the candlelight. Overhead, leftover Christmas decorations read: "Peace on Earth, Good Will to Men."

Charles Eastman, a Sioux who was a government doctor at the agency, worked all night to try to save the wounded

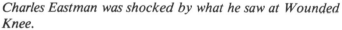

Charles Eastman was shocked by what he saw at Wounded Knee.

Indians. His fiancée, Elaine Goodale, brought in quilts to make the wounded as warm and comfortable as possible.

In the morning a blizzard buried the bodies at Wounded Knee in a frozen white shroud. Two days later a search party was able to make its way back to the camp. Sioux death songs and wailings filled the air as the people found the bodies of their loved ones in the snow. Dr. Eastman came to search for survivors. Surprisingly, some of the Sioux were still alive. The young doctor found a blind old woman under a wagon, unhurt except for frostbite. And wrapped in a blanket beside her fallen mother, he found a crying baby girl. It was a sight the young Sioux doctor would remember all his life.

By the time of Big Foot's capture, most of the Sioux Ghost Dancers were headed back to the reservation. They had been driven out of their Badlands hideout by the winter cold, starvation, and the U.S. Army. Even the strongest believers in the dance, Short Bull and Kicking Bear, decided to surrender.

When these Sioux heard about the Wounded Knee massacre, however, many changed their minds. What if a massacre awaited them, too? In their anger, some Sioux took revenge for Wounded Knee by attacking agency buildings. Soon, however, they were trapped by the army and forced to give themselves up. By mid-January, all the Sioux had been pushed back onto the reservation.

In the war to stop the Ghost Dance, hundreds of Sioux had been killed. But Wounded Knee killed more than just the Indians who died there. The Sioux nation, and, in a sense, the hopes and dreams of all American Indians died at Wounded Knee.

CHAPTER VIII

End Of
The Dream

As the spring of 1891 came to Mason Valley, the Paiutes danced and waited. The promised new world, however, failed to appear. Instead, the white settlers remained on Paiute land. Wovoka's people were deeply disappointed. And their disappointment turned to sorrow when they heard the tragic news of Wounded Knee.

Still hopeful for the coming of the new world, Wovoka set another date for a few weeks later. That date came and went, and yet another later that summer. By August of 1891, the Paiute prophet stopped making predictions. But Wovoka did not give up his belief in the message of the Great Spirit. He encouraged his people to go on dancing.

Outside Mason Valley, most Indians stopped dancing after they heard about Wounded Knee. Tens of thousands lost their faith in the Paiute Messiah. Within a few years, the dance was done in just a few places by small numbers of Indians. Wovoka was little known except among his own people.

At the height of the Ghost Dance in 1890, Wovoka was well known to the whites. They had watched as the dance-in-a-circle swept across the country. Many had been fascinated by the dance, but few had really understood its meaning. They had been afraid that it would cause an Indian uprising. Officials had been most worried about an outbreak among the Sioux. They paid little attention to the faraway Paiute leader whose message had given hope to the Indian world.

Following the tragedy at Wounded Knee, Wovoka stayed away from white people. He felt partly to blame because his teachings had caused the Sioux to start dancing. For a while he would not answer any questions from whites about the dance movement. Then one day, a white stranger came to talk to the Paiute prophet. The stranger, James Mooney, had traveled two thousand miles to learn about the Ghost Dance and the man who had started it.

Mooney was a scientist who studied groups of people from different races and cultures. He had become interested in American Indians as a schoolboy in Indiana. In 1885 he had been hired by the Bureau of American Ethnology in Washington, D.C., to study Indian ways of life. Five years later he was sent out by the bureau to learn about the Ghost Dance.

Though Mooney was white, he understood the problems of American Indians. His parents had come to the United States from Ireland in the mid-1800s. Like the Indians, the Irish were mistreated by other Americans. From the time he was born in 1861, James Mooney was part of an unwanted minority group. At this time the Irish were outnumbered by the millions of other immigrants who had come to America before them. They had to struggle to get fair treatment and equal rights. Perhaps growing up in such a world made James Mooney aware of the problems of other minority groups. Mooney wanted to do more than just study the dance movement. He wanted to find out what it meant to the Indian people.

By the time he arrived in Mason Valley, the young white scientist had already studied the dance among the Plains Indians of Oklahoma, Wyoming, and the Dakotas. In each place he began by making friends with the Indians. He would live with them for months and observe the dance-in-a-circle closely. Few whites had ever won the friendship of so many Indians. And no white person had learned as much about the dance as Mooney.

Still, his study of the dance would not be complete until he questioned Wovoka. In January 1892, Mooney befriended Wovoka's uncle, Charley Sheep. Charley agreed to take the scientist out to Wovoka's camp.

As they neared Wovoka's home, they came upon him hunting in the midst of snow-covered sagebrush. At first Wovoka said very little. But when he found out that Mooney knew many of his friends among the Plains Indians, he greeted him with a warm handshake. That evening he introduced Mooney to his wife and four-year-old son.

The more they talked, the more Wovoka liked the white scientist. The Paiute prophet was glad to find a white person who really wanted to understand the dance-in-a-circle. So many white people had misunderstood it, he told Mooney. Even Indians like the Sioux had made changes in the dance after their visit to Mason Valley. He had given them a dance of peace. They had changed it into a dance of revenge against the whites. That was not the dance that the Great Spirit had given to his people, Wovoka told his guest. The dance had been given to the Indians to give them joy in waiting for the new world.

Wovoka explained to Mooney how the dance movement had begun in Mason Valley. He described the day the sun died and his visions of the new world for Indians. He told about the Indians who had come from far away to learn about the dance. Sadly, he told how he had set the date for the coming of the new world. His story ended with the tragic events at Wounded Knee.

Mooney became such good friends with Wovoka that the Paiute prophet allowed him to take his picture—the first one ever taken of him. He gave his young white friend some sacred red paint, piñon nuts, and magpie feathers to take back to Wovoka's friends among the Plains Indians. When Mooney left Mason Valley, he also took with him an understanding of the dance and its creator that would surprise and anger many whites.

After visiting Wovoka, James Mooney wrote a report about the dance movement. In it he reported that the Paiutes still lived much as their ancestors had lived. They had taken on some of the white people's ways. But they still depended on the plants and animals of their desert home for food. Their houses were the same wickiups made of a frame covered by sagebrush or rushes.

Mooney reported that the Paiutes went on dancing. They danced for the time when the earth would be theirs again, and their ancestors would come back to life. All Indians, they still believed, would one day live happily in a world without whites. No date, however, was set for the coming of the new world.

The U.S. Congress asked James Mooney for a report

about the dance movement. He spoke in favor of the dance and of the rights of American Indians. Many whites complained that he was too much on the side of the Indians. Other accounts of the Ghost Dance had been written by whites who did not understand it. Mooney corrected those one-sided reports with his open-minded, scientific study. He pointed out that Wovoka's dance was a dance of peace, not war. It expressed a vision of hope, he said, for Indians who had lost their lands and their freedom.

At the time Mooney visited Wovoka, the Paiute prophet was just thirty-six years old. He lived many years after the events of Wounded Knee. During the 1890s, Wovoka's fame slowly faded out. In later years few people would remember him except the Paiutes of Mason Valley. Wovoka never gave up his belief in the dance, and he went on teaching it to the Paiutes. He lived a quiet and peaceful life for forty years until his death in 1932. Thousands of Indians had once worshipped him. Only a few were aware of his death.

Today many of Wovoka's descendants make their living by raising cattle and fishing the lakes of western Nevada. Paiutes are still forced to struggle for land and water rights in their homeland. And for the Paiutes who depend on the fish of Pyramid Lake, it has been a losing struggle until recent years.

For centuries the cutthroat trout was an important source of food for the Pyramid Lake Paiutes. In 1905 the whites built Derby Dam over the Truckee River. White farmers wanted the water from the river to irrigate their crops. Cutting off the main source of water for the lake

*Wovoka as an old man
in the 1920s.*

caused its water to turn salty. That, in turn, destroyed the trout's spawning grounds. Each year the level of the lake dropped until it was ninety feet below its normal level. Finally the cutthroat trout disappeared.

In their peaceful and quiet way, the Paiutes struggled to regain the rights to their waters and land. They took their case to the public and the courts. After years of legal battles, the Paiutes began to win support for their rights. During the 1970s the courts ordered the water level raised in Pyramid Lake. Now the lake is restocked with trout each year. The cutthroat trout, however, will never be seen again.

The Paiutes' quiet battle for their rights will go on for years to come. Developers want to use the land around Pyramid Lake to serve white tourists. Already the lake is attracting many fishermen. They come to fish for the trout which the Paiutes need for food.

The Paiutes are still among the poorest of American Indians. Like their ancestors, they work hard to survive in their barren land. Here and there, some Paiutes still dance, much as they did in Wovoka's day. They dance in the hope that one day their homeland will belong to them again. The dream of the coming of the new world is not dead. Time cannot be turned backward—and yet, the people go on dancing.

The photographs are reproduced through the courtesy of:
Burlington Northern; California State Library; Field Museum of
Natural History, George Catlin, artist; Lick Observatory; Nevada
Historical Society; Ohio Historical Society; Seattle Historical
Society; Smithsonian Institution National Anthropological
Archives, Bureau of American Ethnology Collection; South Dakota
Historical Society; South Dakota Tourism Division; Steve Ask; and
the University of Nevada Library, Reno.

THE AUTHOR

Mel Boring is a free-lance writer whose stories and articles for children have appeared in many magazines. He is the author of four books, including *Sealth: The Story of an American Indian*, published by Dillon Press. Until recently, he taught in elementary, junior high, and high schools in Kansas, Michigan, California, and Vermont. During his teaching career, Mr. Boring also wrote and edited audiovisual mathematics and metrics programs. A graduate of Sterling College in Kansas, Mel now lives in Santa Barbara, California, with his wife, Carol, and two sons, Josh and Jeremy.

OTHER BIOGRAPHIES
IN THIS SERIES ARE